Usborne
First Sticker Book

...and lots of other ENORMOUS dinosaurs

Illustrated by
Diego Vaisberg

You'll find all the stickers and a word list at the back of the book.

Contents

2 King of the dinosaurs
4 A fishy feast
6 Fierce fighters
8 Midnight snack
10 Humungous herbivore
12 On the hunt
14 Gentle giants
16 Where are they now?

Words by Alice Beecham   Designed by Maddison Warnes
With expert advice from Rhys Charles,
The Bristol Dinosaur Project

King of the dinosaurs 68-66 million years ago

The Tyrannosaurus rex is one of the biggest and fiercest **predators** that has ever lived. These huge **carnivores** had 60 bone-crushing teeth, and the strongest bite of any land animal ever discovered.

Stick on a T. rex choosing its next **prey**.

Fill this page with dinosaurs trying to escape.

A fishy feast

95-94 million years ago

The Spinosaurus was as big as a T. rex, but preferred to eat fish. Spinosaurus had crocodile-like jaws, perfect for snapping up slippery sea creatures.

Stick a fishing Spinosaurus on the shore.

Add a Carcharodontosaurus looking for some lunch.

Stick on a Kaprosuchus, basking in the sun.

Fierce fighters 68-66 million years ago

T. rexes sometimes fought each other. They could bite so hard that they left holes in their enemies' bones.

Add lots of smaller dinosaurs fleeing from the fight.

Stick on two battling T. rexes.

Midnight snack 68-66 million years ago

Tiny Dakotaraptors were much too small to try to fight a T. rex. Instead, these sneaky little dinosaurs are stealing eggs from the T. rex nests while the parents are sleeping.

Fill this nest with tasty T. rex eggs.

Stick lots of stealthy
Dakotaraptors on this page.

Humungous herbivore 95 million years ago

This enormous dinosaur is a Patagotitan. Even the largest predators, like the Giganotosaurus, were tiny in comparison to these massive **herbivores**. Find some **carnivorous** dinosaurs to fight this Patagotitan.

Stick on a Giganotosaurus getting walloped by the Patagotitan's tail.

Add some Argentinadracos
swooping through the sky.

On the hunt 68-66 million years ago

Some dinosaurs had sharp horns and clubbed tails that made them difficult to hunt. Clever T. rexes might have worked together to try to take them down.

Add a mother Triceratops protecting her baby.

Stick on an Ankylosaurus
fighting back against
an angry T. rex.

Gentle giants 145 million years ago

Some **herbivorous** dinosaurs towered over the biggest carnivores. Add a Diplodocus, a Brachiosaurus and a Supersaurus to this scene, and some smaller dinosaurs too.

Stick another Stegosaurus by this stream.

Add a grazing
Gargoyleosaurus here.

Where are they now?

All the dinosaurs in this book lived millions of years ago. Over time, their bodies were buried under layers of earth, and turned into **fossils**. Add the missing T. rex bones to this picture.

Stick on another **paleontologist** studying some bones.

Word list

Carnivore – an animal that only eats meat
Carnivorous – meat-eating
Fossil – the remains of an animal or plant that have turned into rock over a very long time
Herbivore – an animal that only eats plants
Herbivorous – plant-eating
Paleontologist – someone who studies fossils to learn about the past
Predator – an animal that hunts and eats other animals
Prey – an animal that is hunted by a predator

King of the dinosaurs

pages 2–3

A fishy feast

pages 4–5

Fierce fighters

pages 6–7

Midnight snack

pages 8–9

Humungous herbivore

pages 10–11

On the hunt pages 12–13

Gentle giants
pages 14–15
Diplodocus
Brachiosaurus
Gargoyleosaurus
Supersaurus
Stegosaurus

Where are they now?

page 16

You can use these stickers anywhere.